Money Management Mindset

7 Strategies to Financial Management

Israel Duran

ISRAEL DURAN
Become The Solution

Disclaimer: The author and publisher of this book and the accompanying materials have used their best efforts in preparing this book. The author and publisher make no representation or warranties with respect to the accuracy, applicability, fitness or completeness of the contents of this book. The information contained in this book is strictly for educational purposes. Therefore, if you wish you apply ideas contained in this book you are taking full responsibility for your actions.

Israel Duran & Associates, LLC

Visit our websites:
www.israelduran.com
www.israelduran.org

ISBN: 978-0-578-21242-5

CONTENTS

INTRODUCTION

Are you in debt and struggling to pay the bills? Do you wish you had more time to do the things that you love to do? Are you struggling to manage your finances and desire additional help? If you answered yes to any of these questions, then this book is right for you. About 80% of the U.S population is in debt; many snared into massive debt and unable to overcome it because of the lack of financial education. You cannot apply to your life what you do not know nor understand. If I would have known what I know now about financial management, I probably would have taken another route to pursue higher education, rather than accumulating student loan debt. With a Bachelor's in Criminal Justice and a Master's in Cyber Security, I assure you I know a little bit about student loan debt.

Growing up, I didn't have anyone to teach me about avoiding bad debt or financial management principles. Maybe you can relate. Many of the principles I am going to share in this book have come from my learning experiences and failures. A man once said, "Sometimes you win, and sometimes you learn." In life, challenges are learning opportunities that can set you up for greatness.

Today, there is a growing problem of what I call the debt cycle. The debt cycle is a trap of getting into more and more debt without being able to pay it off. I believe that part of this debt cycle is due to a lack of education and knowledge with regards to financial management. In this book, my desire is to provide you with some strategies to unlocking financial success that will equip you to manage your finances and ultimately help you reach your financial goals.

Many families are struggling due to this lack of financial education. In 2018, Americans' total credit card debt continues to climb, reaching an estimated $927 billion, a more than 5% increase from the previous year. It is surprising to note that the average household that's carrying credit card debt has a balance of $15,482. On average, households with any kind of debt owe $134,058 (including mortgages). Student loans are continuing to rise as the average debt per American is $46,950. It is clear that something needs to be done, in order to help individuals and families get out of bad debt and manage their finances.

Type of debt	Total owed by average US household carrying this type of debt	Total debt owed by US consumers
Credit cards	$15,482	$927 billion
Mortgages	$181,176	$9 trillion
Auto Loans	$27,669	$1.24 trillion
Student Loans	$46,950	$1.41 trillion
Any Type of Debt	$134,058	$13.29 trillion

Debt balances are current as of June 2018 Source - NerdWallet. Com

CHAPTER 1

A STRATEGY TO UNDERSTANDING MONEY

If you grew up in America, the odds are you probably did not receive any financial education. This is due to the flawed education system America has developed. It is important to note that most schools in America do not teach financial literacy. The focus is teaching you to get a job. In other words, the educational system in America teaches students to be slaves to a job, to work for money. I pose a question to you; do you really want to work for someone else your whole life? If not, then financial literacy will be extremely beneficial to you for self-development, in order to accomplish your life goals.

Due to this flawed educational system, it is very rare to see someone who manages their finances well at an early age, unless their parents taught them while growing up. However, parents who are teaching their children about finances are the minority. There are more people who grow up in homes where parents are not financially literate or have trouble managing their own finances. For instance, there are many in America who have immigrant parents who work hard, laboring for 20 to 40 years and after have nothing or little to show for it. It is the lack of education or ignorance that leads people to make wrong decisions in certain areas of life. Therefore, it is important when talking about financial management to clearly define the function of money. The first strategy is simply educating on the function of money. By defining the function of money, it will hopefully give you more insight on how money works. In result equipping you to better manage your finances.

What is the Function of Money?

In today's world, there is nothing that money can't answer. You have probably heard the saying in this world "there's nothing that money can't buy." The reason I use the word "answer" instead of "buy" is because money is used in the marketplace. People use the money to exchange goods and services. The "function of money" has always been around. The "function of money" pre-dates when currency came into use.

In early civilizations, people traded goods and resources such as corn, tomatoes, and wheat, in exchange for other goods or services. The function of money was still at work even though money, as we know it today, was not. In the marketplace, one would trade animals for spices or spices for animals. The function of money was at work with resources, but in today's civilization, we use paper currency. We still see some forms of trade for resources such as food and water, but for the most part, in today's day and age, money is usually traded for goods and services.

It is important to define the function of money when seeking to understand money itself. As seen in our world today, money is there to provide goods and services to humanity. If there was no money in the world, things would be chaotic. But because money is in the world, it helps governments govern and keeps people in order, to live stable lives. For example, America is a capitalist nation, you have the right to work to reach financial success. This financial success would not be possible if money was not a part of society.

The Two Extremes of Money

When I think about the extremes of money, I think about having the right balance. Balance is something that we all need in life. Without it, it is very easy to go to an extreme. Extremes can hinder us from developing ourselves and moving forward in life. The world today is full of extremes in many different categories, but especially with money. That is why in the following pages, I will illustrate the two extremes of money, both of which are rooted in human nature. Once you understand these two extremes, which is sometimes buried in your subconscious or conscious mind, you will be better equipped to avoid them. Again, the goal of going over these two extremes is to help you better steward your finances.

First Extreme - Money is the Root of All Evil

Have you ever heard someone say, "money is the root of all evil?" You probably have, but unfortunately, people misquote this biblical verse often. It actually states that "**the love of money** is the root of all evil." Money in itself is harmless, neutral, and usually in a form of paper, which came from a tree. But the love or greed of money is what leads people to do horrible things to obtain or hoard it. Part of this is due to the lack of understanding people have with regards to money. People who love money do not understand the function of money as written before. This lack of understanding and ignorance is what causes people to commit horrible things for money. This is the first extreme of money that needs to be avoided if one desires to get out of debt, one needs to become free from the "love of money."

Second Extreme - The Poverty Mindset

The other extreme of money that needs to be avoided is embracing poverty or lack of money as something that is good. The poverty mindset is somehow embedded in our culture today. It is the other extreme that hinders people from managing their finances properly. It assumes every rich person to be evil. With this false perspective in the minds of many, it is difficult for many to deliver themselves from this lie which is holding them from being free financially. Persons with the poverty mindset believe that there is not enough money in the world for everyone. This just simply isn't true.

There is a Bible verse that declares the way you judge others is how you will be judged. The poverty mindset leads people to judge and say horrible things about people who have money, causing them to be bound by their own words. Imagine a person who speaks poorly of a rich person, claiming they should give that money all away, or they are evil because they have money. As this individual is subconsciously releasing these thoughts and passing judgment, they are limiting themselves from being financially healthy as well. For example, we have all heard someone say something about the wealthy such as "they should do this or that with their money." It is no wonder that they are struggling with their finances. This is why it is important to renew your mind from this false view. This extreme is what causes people to waste and mismanage money.

Whatever You Fail to Manage

Both extremes have a common outcome. This outcome is the number one reason why many individuals are failing to manage their finances properly. This outcome is what I like to call the **"disrespect of money."** Both of these extremes- having a love of money or embracing the lack of money- produce a disrespect of money in one's life. When someone loses respect for anything, it will lose its value to that individual. When something loses its value to someone, that individual will eventually fail to manage it; **whatever you fail to manage you will lose.** If you do not manage your finances you will find yourself in debt, with no assets, and probably stressed. This is why it is important to properly understand money and its function. It is necessary to overcome the ignorance that leads people to mismanage gifts, talents, and money in their lives. In other words, you need to develop a respect for money, not a love for money, so you can properly manage it.

Renewal of Your Mind About Money

Renewing your mind about anything in life is the first step to correctly changing bad behavior. You can see why I had to properly lay the foundation before going into some principles and strategies that will help you achieve your financial success. Poor financial management has little to do with the amount of money you are making, it starts with your mindset.

Every self-made millionaire properly handled their finances to get to where they are. Many millionaires started off completely broke, showing that your mindset is more important than your circumstances. It is unfortunate that many people are subconsciously or consciously having thoughts towards money that create a disrespect of money in their lives, which lead them in mismanagement. Let's change that by becoming the solution to poor management by choosing to manage the gifts, talents, and money that come into our lives.

CHAPTER 2

A STRATEGY TO PROPER GOAL SETTING

There was a boy who set a goal to win a championship race for his late father. This boy had a passion for sports and his track career. Before this boy's father passed away, he made a promise to his father that he would win a championship race for him. Fast forward two years, this boy had the opportunity to compete in the state final. POP! The sound of the gun went off and this boy went off to the races. When the race started the boy was off to a good start, but halfway through the race his knee started to hurt. This boy was in place to finish second or third and in extreme pain, but because this boy had made a promise to his father, he decided to push himself, even with all the pain he was experiencing. That boy finished in first place like he had promised his father.

Determining Your Why

What is the why that will allow you to finish the race even when it hurts? This boy's story teaches us a great principle that we should all apply to our lives. This is a principle that I would like to release to you. Your why needs to be bigger than your now. When it comes to managing your finances, things will happen to try and discourage you from pressing forward. I encourage you to ask yourself what is my why? Why is it that you want to get out of bad debt? Why do you want financial freedom? What's the point? You're going to need to look into yourself and get to the root answer. This root answer is your why and is needed for when the difficult moments arise. This is the principle that unlocks the strategy to proper goal setting and setting yourself up for success.

The Passion Within You

I like to refer to your why as the passion within you. It is the fuel that allows you to keep going forward. Determining your why connects to your vision. Your vision is where you are headed, where is your why taking you? To accomplish your vision, there is a critical attribute that is needed and that is discipline. Discipline is an important factor when seeking to execute on your goals while chasing your vision. But what is equally important as vision is discipline, because having discipline will allow you to execute your vision and reach the success you desire!

An example of this is one you may have heard of. The Bible declares that Jesus Christ, the son of God, endured the cross because of the joy set before Him (Hebrews 12:2). Jesus Himself went through the pain, suffering, and agony of death on the cross because of His why. His why, His vision was to see humanity reconciled back to God and have the opportunity to have their sins forgiven through His life, death, burial, and resurrection. Jesus' goal was to bring back the Kingdom of God to humankind.

You see, this concept of determining your why needs to be clear within you when trying to change and accomplish your goals. Discipline needs to be a foundational principle that you are applying in your life. Regardless of what your goal is, if your why is greater than what you will go through, then you will be an overcomer and accomplish your goals!

CHAPTER 3

A STRATEGY TO KNOWING YOUR INCOME & EXPENSES

Now that we had laid a proper foundation of understanding the function of money and determining your why for reaching your goals, we are ready to get more in-depth with your individual finances. Applying a strategy to knowing your income and expenses will unlock the information you need to successfully manage your finances.

When we discuss financial management, it is important to understand what our current financial situation is and what money we have available to us. As mentioned in the introduction "you cannot apply to your life what you do not know nor understand." This is a foundation truth that leads to a strategy of knowing your income and expenses. Surprisingly many individuals who are struggling with their finances are not aware of their full income or expenses. How can we effectively manage our finances, if we are not aware of what we actually have? Therefore, let us discuss the Income and Expense statement.

Understanding Cash Flow

An income and expense statement represents the inflow of money (i.e. income) to an individual and the outflow of money (i.e. expenses). I recommend everyone that is looking to better manage their finances to use an income and expense statement. This applies if they are single or married. I recommend this because instead of implementing just a budget, an individual must treat themselves like they are running a business. It is a business of their life. An Income and Expense statement helps an individual better steward and keep an account of what they have been producing and spending. This statement is important for every individual because it will lead us to properly understand what negative or positive cash flow is left at the end of the month. Cash flow is defined as income minus expenses. This number can be either positive or negative. A reason why people get into more debt each year is because of a negative cash flow.

To create your income and expense statement:

1. Write down all your monthly Income; if you are married, do this with your spouse.

2. Write down all your monthly Expenses

3. Subtract your monthly Expenses from your monthly Income

4. This is your Positive or Negative Cash Flow

See example below of the proper equation:

1. *Monthly Income: $3700*
2. *Monthly Expenses: $2550*
3. *Positive Monthly Cash Flow: $1150*

Now that you have identified your monthly cash flow number. We can now use this when we discuss how to master a budget. This cash flow number is what you really make, after all necessary expenses. What you do with this positive cash flow will determine whether your finances will be managed properly or poorly.

CHAPTER 4

A STRATEGY TO MASTERING A BUDGET

Many times, we hear of budgeting, but we never sit down to study what a budget actually is. In this chapter, my desire is to explain the purpose of a budget and share some tools that you can apply to your life to improve your budgeting. A budget is important when managing our finances. It serves as a plan or estimate for your monthly cash flow to be properly managed.

Automatic Savings

Having a budget is an important strategy when thinking about saving any money for future investments and or goals. Once you identify your positive cash flow and sit down to properly plan what you will do with your positive cash flow, savings will always come to mind. I recommend using a percentage to determine how much you will save from your monthly positive cash flow. Now, this is not a set amount of what you should save. This is totally up to your discernment and goals. I recommend saving 20-30% of your positive cash flow.

If you have a 401K plan with your employer, I would recommend saving at least 7% of your salary. Remember once you set your 401K deductions, they are automatic and are taken out of your paycheck before the IRS taxes you. In other words, you are saving more of your hard-earned money. I recommend 7% but whatever percentage you choose to save automatically remember this is a strategy that will help you prepare and plan for your future. It is also important to note that there are other alternatives to a 401K which I would highly recommend, but the important principle is that you are saving automatically.

Automatic savings will take the task of moving money over to another account immediately. I would also recommend paying expenses like this as well. For example, your mortgage or rent, car insurance, cell phone, or small utilities. This will help you save time and meet your budget. There are countless programs that enable you to save money automatically and also invest it for you. Master your budget by setting up automatic payments and a savings plan that fits your budget. Remember having an automatic savings system in your financial planning will save you time and money.

It is also important to have an emergency fund of at least $1,500 when thinking about budgeting. This fund should have easy access for when a true emergency arises. It's better to be prepared in case something does occur than to be caught off guard and go into debt to pay for an emergency. Many financial experts recommend having 6 – 10 months' worth of living expenses saved just a case of a serious emergency.

Money Allocation Diagram

Allocation is the action or process of distributing something. Money needs to be distributed properly when planning a budget. I have created a money allocation diagram for business owners that outlines the proper allocation for effective financial management. If you are not a business owner, this diagram is still for you. Just change the allocation percentages to what best fits you. I recommend percentages of 10|30|60, which simplifies the allocation in personal finances: 10% for the tithe, as it is important to give when seeking financial success; 30% is for paying off debt, saving and investment; and 60% for living expenses.

Example Money Allocation Diagram

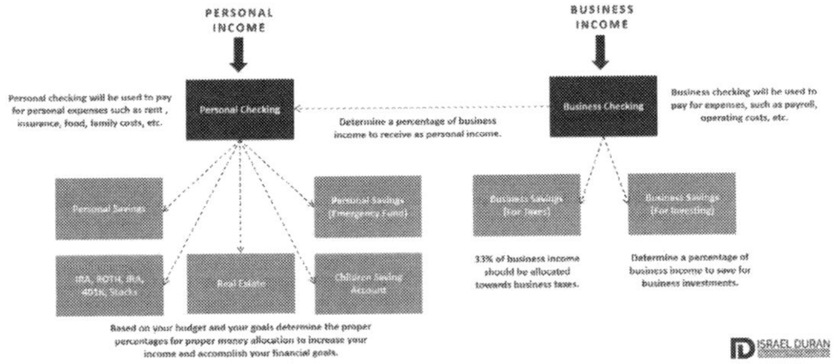

CHAPTER 5

A STRATEGY TO GETTING OUT OF BAD DEBT

There is a saying that states "before something was big, it was small." In other words, to get to the big you must first focus on the small. When it comes to getting out of debt, most people get discouraged because they look at the great amounts that they owe and overlook the small amounts they owe. This is why when some people go to the store, they don't care about picking up small items such as a chocolate bar and some gum. In peoples mind they say, well it's only a dollar, and after all a few dollars won't make a difference, right? If those few extra bucks go toward paying off your debt each month you would be better off financially.

When setting up a plan to pay off bad debt, it is important to focus on your small debts first and then the big ones. This statement is the foundation to a strategy I call the debt accelerator. This strategy is designed to help you eliminate debt at a rapid pace. This is why I call it the debt accelerator since it is a strategy to accelerate debt elimination. Let's say you have 4 different credit cards you want to pay off. The first credit card you owe is $400, the second $800, the third $2000, and the fourth is $5000. The debt accelerator will allow you to make consistent payments on all your debts. The debt that we suggest you pay off first is called your target account. This would be the first credit card because it carries the lowest amount of debt. Once we pay off the target account, you roll over the amount you were paying toward your next target account. As each debt is paid off, you continue this process.

The debt accelerator allows you to make the same total monthly payment each month toward all your debt and works best when you do not accrue any new debts. This process continues until you have paid off all your debts. It is exciting when you knock out each debt because your debt elimination gets accelerated. Paying off the smallest debt also keeps you motivated to continue. When you finish paying off your debts, you can apply the amount you were paying towards your debt toward creating wealth and financial independence!

Good Debt versus Bad Debt

It is exciting to have a plan of getting out of bad debt, but how can you understand what the difference is between bad and good debt? Defining bad and good debt will give you a better understanding of implementing the debt accelerator in your life.

Good debt is debt that makes you money or increases your monthly cash flow. An example of good debt would be business debt. An example of business debt would be getting a business loan to buy inventory, in order to sell and increase sales. Although you are borrowing capital, it is for expansion and increasing sales. Bad debt is defined as debt that costs you money or decreases your monthly cash flow. The best example of bad debt is personal credit card debt. Credit card debt is usually known for high-interest rates, these high interests' rate is costing you more money to use the credit card itself. This form of debt doesn't make you money, but it cost you money. When defining bad debt and good debt it is important to also explain the difference between assets and liabilities.

Understanding Assets and Liabilities

Good debt and bad debt are closely tied to better understanding assets and liabilities. Assets are defined as items that are owned and have value, which increases your monthly cash flow. In my opinion, an asset is anything that would increase your income, such as a multi-family home, which brings you some extra income monthly that you are renting out, or perhaps stock investments in the stock market that pay dividends. A dividend is a payment of profits that is divided among all the shareholders of a company. Many individuals use their dividends to either reinvest in that stock or use the profits to pay off existing debt.

Liabilities are defined as obligations or items that are owed to others. Liabilities are the complete opposite of assets. An example of a liability could be a single-family home that you haven't paid in full. The mortgage is a liability since it increases your monthly expenses. Alternatively, a multi-family home would bring you extra income monthly, while a single-family home that isn't paid off completely, costs you money. When thinking about the debt accelerator it is vital to think about where we are spending our money. Are we spending our money on liabilities or are we spending our money investing in assets?

CHAPTER 6

A STRATEGY TO RESTORING YOUR CREDIT SCORE

As mentioned in the introduction, debt is extremely high in America today, and debt directly affects the credit scores of many. Today, the credit scores of many individuals are at an extreme low, due to the lack of education of how credit works. If people do not know or understand credit, they will not be able to properly use it. Since few educational systems are teaching about credit score and how credit works, what can we expect, except poor management of credit.

Therefore, it is important to include this chapter, it will help educate you on credit and how it works, as well as giving you a strategy to help restore your credit score and maintain it. This is another important strategy to implement on your road to unlocking financial success! A lot of individuals think that restoring or maintaining good credit is not needed when you have money, but the following paragraphs will explain why it is important.

When we think about financial management, we

need to express the importance of credit. Credit is the ability of a customer to obtain goods or services before payment, based on trust that payment will be made in the future. It is important not to use credit to get further into debt, but rather be responsible if your credit score is low due to unpaid debts. Having integrity is key when restoring your credit score because you want to be in good standing with anyone that you owe.

The Three Credit Reporting Agencies

There are three different major credit reporting agencies that maintain a record of your credit history known as your credit report. Those three are Experian Credit Bureau, TransUnion®, and Equifax®. Your credit score is based on the information in your credit report at the time it is requested. There are several websites and organizations online where you can obtain your credit. One website, CreditKarma.com, provides a free credit monitoring service that I would recommend for starters. There's no trial subscription and you'll never have to give your credit card number. Credit Karma allows you to monitor your TransUnion and Equifax credit report score at no cost.

At CreditKarma.com your credit report information is updated weekly. Along with monitoring of your credit score, you can receive alerts when unusual activity is suspected on either of your two credit reports.

While the service is free, one of the drawbacks if that you won't get access to one of your credit reports and credit scores. You'll have to use another service to monitor your third credit report from Experian. This is not a problem because Experian.com has a trial subscription where you can obtain your score from them.

The Seven Factors of Credit

Once you obtain your credit scores from Credit Karma, look them over and identify what is negatively impacting your credit score, as well as what is positively impacting your credit score. The seven main factors or areas that affect your credit are the following:

1. Payment history
2. Public records
3. Length of credit history
4. New accounts
5. Inquiries
6. Accounts in use
7. Credit Mix and Types

I would encourage you to plan action steps for each factor that is negatively impacting your credit score. Do this is the order from the first factor to the seventh factor. Go over each of these areas within your credit reports and highlight areas where you can improve. For example, go over your payment history and start to pay the minimum monthly payment on time if you aren't already doing so. If you have any accounts in collections that are hitting your public records, reach out to the organization to come up with a payment plan. Sometimes they are willing to negotiate for an agreed settlement amount. Go over each area and correct the root cause of your credit being decreased. Once you go over these seven main areas of your credit score, including paying your debt on time, your credit score will start to improve. This will get you moving in the right direction of restoring your credit score. Remember integrity is a foundational principle when restoring anything in life.

The Importance of Leveraged Credit

Now you have a strategy to improve and restore your credit score. It is important to have a strategy to implement your credit score when managing and stewarding your finances. Today credit is used almost for everything. For example, when applying to rent out an apartment, the landlord usually requests a credit score, to see if you can be approved for the apartment. When applying to jobs, more and more employers are checking potential employees credit score. I hope you can see the importance of leveraging credit in your life.

Let us look at an example of two individuals. Person number 1 has a good credit score and has been faithful in paying back his debtors or people that he owes. Person number 2 hasn't been faithful in paying off debt and has accumulated a lot of credit card debt which has directly affected his credit score. Imagine if both persons were applying for the same job and had the same qualifications for the job. Who do you think will stand out between the two if the employer is checking for credit score to measure integrity? Person number 1 would stand out and have a better likelihood in landing the job. I write this to encourage you to take the steps of restoring your credit, this will help you leverage your credit while seeking to better manage your finances!

CHAPTER 7

A Strategy to Producing Money

Someone once said that money does not grow on trees. However, fruits come from trees, and if you sell the fruit that falls off the tree you can earn money. In other words, money can come from trees. I like to share this because it highlights perspective and mindset. In this chapter, I will share a strategy that will allow you to produce money. Or rather, some principles that will help unlock ideas and change your perspective about how you can produce money.

Business Creation

Creativity is a concept that this world lacks. We are taught from birth to do things a certain way, and if you don't do it this way you are wrong. I believe this ideology is hindering society today because it limits the potential of our creativity. For this reason, I am writing about business creation. Business creation is the strategy to producing money and building wealth. A business is defined as the activity of making one's living or making money by producing or buying and selling products (goods and services). Simply put, a business solves problems either through a product or service and produces money through that system.

When developing your finances having a business is foundational to increase productivity and building wealth. This is because a business can be a system that works for you to solve problems or meet a need. A business can become an asset that brings you monthly income. A business can increase productivity in your life compared to just having a 9 to 5 job. There are endless opportunities when you have a system that works for you, compared to being limited in a job from 9-5. Having a 9-5 is not bad, but it does not allow you to be productive for yourself, you are building someone else's dream. This is why I encourage each of you that are reading this book because you have talents, gifts, and passions that can be used in business to solve problems or meet peoples needs. When you solve these problems and serve people, money will find you; and that is a strategy!

Solution Development

Solving a problem sounds easy to the ear, but this world faces a lot of problems. From political, to social, religious and governmental problems, this world needs you to stand up with solutions and lead the way to better change. Why not help become a solution to a problem and release your full potential on earth? This is why solution development is another principle of making money. What is the point of having a lot of money, but not helping anyone with the abundance? I tell you the truth, money goes to those who solve problems and those who meet people's needs. In my life, I live by the principle of seeking God's kingdom first and His righteousness. By me seeking God's government, I am becoming part of the solution to this world, because the kingdom of God is the solution to mankind's problems. In life, we all need to decide whether we will be part of this world's problems or we will be part of this world's solution.

I encourage you to think about a problem that you encountered in life. I encourage you to think about something that you dislike or hate. Whatever it is, I encourage you to be the difference and become the solution to the problem that you hate. When you identify what you hate, you will identify the problem that you're called to solve. When you start to use your gift to solve those problems in life, the fulfillment you have been seeking will find you. When thinking of making money do not chase money. Rather chase the ideas that solve problems and money will come to you!

Investment Ideas

The idea of investment has always been around.

Investment is when you plant something and subsequently will reap. It has the idea of sowing and harvesting; just think of a seed. When you plant a seed, it takes time for that seed to grow. Likewise, investments do not profit overnight. When thinking about investment ideas, we need to have the mindset of planting and growing. Seeds do not grow in one day, although sometimes when we invest, we hope it does. Our mindset when thinking about producing money with investments should be geared to long-term growth. There are some investment ideas that will give an instant return but usually has a high risk as well. This is due to the fact that high reward usually has high risk attached to it.

When we think about producing money and managing our finances, we need to have the investor's mindset. The planting and harvesting mindset. I encourage you to think about investment ideas. Some types of investments would be stocks, real estate, starting a business, creating a product, etc. There are endless opportunities out there. If you need help brainstorming investment ideas or would like to learn different investment strategies, check out our website at www.IsraelDDuran.com for more resources. Many individuals use investments as a tool or vehicle to become financially free and or to become wealthy. This is possible because investments gain interest which is needed to "grow" money since inflation makes the purchasing power of the dollar go down.

Perhaps this goes hand and hand with business creation and solution development, but investing is when your money is producing money for you. I always encourage individuals to invest in themselves. There is no telling what return you will receive by investing in yourself such as reading books like this. You are reading this book now, but perhaps you will be writing one soon or you are writing one now. Maybe this book will encourage you to think about a multi-million-dollar idea or rather a multi-million-dollar solution. I encourage you to continue to invest in yourself. It is an investment that will pay off when seeking to better manage your finances and reaching a greater level of success.

Just like the seed that has the potential to grow inside of itself, your potential is inside of you. Books or other personal development resources like this help unlock your full potential to release your full potential on earth. You are a solution to this generation. I encourage you to partner up with God and His kingdom to release your purpose and calling on earth!

FINAL THOUGHTS

Principles stay the same, but strategies develop. The principles and strategies that I have shared in this book are important and will stay the same, but the strategies of applying them can vary. I encourage you to apply these principles in your life to better manage your finances. Many people read several books like these but never apply what they learn. Reading is important, but the application is much more important. When you apply these principles to your life and use the strategies that you have learned in this book, they will unlock the potential that is within you.

My desire is that you now have a better understanding of the function and purpose of money on the earth, so you can respect the finances that go through your hands to better manage them. When setting your goals, it is important that your why is bigger than what you will go through to overcome it. Remember that all it takes is an idea or solution to be able to make a difference in this world and produce money for yourself.

To learn more about financial management, debt-free living, or developing a business, make sure to visit my blog on my website! Whether you're a business owner or an individual who would like to develop a business, we have specific services that will help you get to your next level. We offer services for those who need to overcome some hurdles and are looking for one-on-one coaching on how to build a business or develop a business idea. Reach out and let us help you identify the right steps for you to accomplish your vision! Visit https://IsraelDuran.Com/Services and schedule your session today!

Example of Cash Flow Statement – Income and Expenses

Cash Flow - Income / Expense Worksheet

		<-- Enter data in this					<-- Enter data in this column	
GROSS INCOME PER MONTH			$0		9	**Enter./Recreation**		$0
	Salary					Eating Out		
	Interest					Baby Sitters		
	Dividends					Activities/Trips		
	Social Security					Vacation		
	VA Benefits					Other (________)		
						Other (________)		
LESS:								
1	**Tithe|Offering – Rich Toward God**		$0	10% +	10	**Clothing**		$0
2	**Savings – Save to Invest**		$0	5% +	11	**Medical Expenses**		$0
						Doctor		
3	**Tax (Est. – Federal, State, FICA)**		$0			Dentist		
						Orthodontist		
	NET SPENDABLE INCOME		$0			Other		
4	**Housing**		$0		12	**Miscellaneous**		$0
	Mortgage (rent)					Toiletry, cosmetics		
	Insurance					Beauty, Barber		
	Taxes					Laundry, cleaning		
	Electricity					Allowances, Lunches		
	Gas					Subscriptions		
	Water					Gifts (include Christmas)		
	Sanitation					Cash		
	Telephone					Cable/Internet		
	Maintenance					Other (________)		
	Other (________)					Other (________)		
	Other (________)							
					13	**Investments**		$0
5	**Food**		$0					
					14	**School / Child Care**		$0
6	**Automobiles**		$0			Tuition		
	Payments					Materials		
	Gas and Oil					Transportation		
	Insurance					Day Care		
	License/Taxes					Other (________)		
	Maintenance/Repair							
	Replace					**TOTAL EXPENSES**		$0
7	**Insurance**		$0		**INCOME VERSUS EXPENSES**			
	Life					**Net Spendable Income**		$0
	Medical					**Less Expenses**		$0
	Other (________)					**Positive or Negative CASH FLOW**		$0
8	**Debts**		$0		15	**Unallocated Surplus Income**		
	Credit Card							
	Loans and Notes							
	Other (________)							
	Other (________)							

15 - This category is used when surplus income is received. This would remain in the checking account to be used within a few weeks; otherwise, it should be transferred to an allocated category.

PAGE OF NOTES

Contact Israel

To interact with Israel through Facebook and Twitter, visit

IsraelDuran.com

If you are interested in learning more visit our blog for free information at

IsraelDuran.com/Blog

To book Israel for a speaking engagement, email

info@israeldduran.com

Made in the USA
Monee, IL
04 November 2026

67382349R00024